D0848297

Snap books®

STAR BIOGRAPHIES

Zac Efron

by Sheila Griffin Llanas

Capstone
press®

Mankato, Minnesota

Snap Books are published by Capstone Press,
151 Good Counsel Drive, P.O. Box 669, Mankato, Minnesota 56002.
www.capstonepress.com

Copyright © 2010 by Capstone Press, a Capstone Publishers company.
All rights reserved.
No part of this publication may be reproduced in whole or in part, or stored in a retrieval system,
or transmitted in any form or by any means, electronic, mechanical, photocopying, recording,
or otherwise, without written permission of the publisher.
For information regarding permission, write to Capstone Press,
151 Good Counsel Drive, P.O. Box 669, Dept. R, Mankato, Minnesota 56002.
Printed in the United States of America

Books published by Capstone Press are manufactured with paper
containing at least 10 percent post-consumer waste.

Library of Congress Cataloging-in-Publication Data
Llanas, Sheila Griffin.
    Zac Efron / by Sheila Griffin Llanas.
    p. cm. — (Snap books. Star biographies)
    Summary: "Describes the life and career of Zac Efron" — Provided by publisher.
    Includes bibliographical references and index.
    Includes webliography.
    ISBN 978-1-4296-3402-1 (library binding)
    1. Efron, Zac — Juvenile literature. 2. Actors — United States — Biography — Juvenile literature. I. Title.
II. Series.
PN2287.E395L35 2010
791.4302'8092 — dc22   2009002749

Editor: Megan Peterson
Designer: Juliette Peters
Media Researcher: Marcie Spence

Photo Credits:
AP Images/Mark J. Terrill, 29; AP Images/Matt Sayles, 23; Corbis/Phil McCarten/Reuters, 21; The Disney Channel/
The Kobal Collection, 17; The Disney Channel/The Kobal Collection/Larkey, Adam, 6; Getty Images Inc./Amy Graves/
WireImage, 28; Getty Images Inc./Dimitrios Kambouris/WireImage, cover; Getty Images Inc./Frazer Harrison, 11; Getty
Images Inc./Jon Furniss/WireImage, 7; Getty Images Inc./Munawar Hosain/Fotos International, 5; Newscom, 9 (school);
Newscom/Jeffrey Thurnher/The WB, 16; Newscom/PacificCoastNews, 9 (Zac); Newscom/SHNS photo courtesy New Line
Cinema, 24; Newscom/Splash News and Pictures, 12, 27; Supplied by Capital Pictures, 15; Walt Disney Pictures/The
Kobal Collection, 18

Essential content words are **bold** and are defined at the bottom of the page where they first appear.

CENTRAL ARKANSAS LIBRARY SYSTEM
CHILDREN'S LIBRARY
LITTLE ROCK, ARKANSAS

Table of Contents

CHAPTER 1

Zac's Biggest Audition

Zac Efron, a little-known 17-year-old actor, liked the movie script his **agent** handed him in 2005. It was called *High School Musical*. Disney producers wanted new faces to star in the made-for-TV movie musical. Zac really wanted the lead role of Troy Bolton, a high school athlete who secretly wants to act. Hundreds of other young actors also wanted the part. Zac had performed in stage musicals and appeared in TV shows. He had even starred in two small movies. But was his experience enough to give him an edge at the **audition**?

agent — someone who helps actors find work
audition — a tryout performance for an actor

Zac starred on TV and in two small movies before his *High School Musical* audition.

The audition was not as simple as reading from a script. Hopeful actors spent an entire day acting, singing, dancing, and playing basketball. For his solo, Zac sang "Let Me Love You" by Mario. The judges liked what they heard. They asked Zac to read dialogue with Vanessa Hudgens, who was trying out for the female lead. Zac and Vanessa had good chemistry. The judges kept them together for the rest of the audition.

Zac and *High School Musical* costar Vanessa Hudgens were paired up at the audition.

One by one, actors felt a tap on the shoulder and were asked to leave the audition. Zac braced for a shoulder tap, but it never came. Finally only one other actor stood between Zac and his dream role. Producers sent the boys home and told them to wait for a phone call. Ten days later, Zac's phone rang. He won the part of Troy Bolton in *High School Musical*. Zac Efron was about to become a household name.

Zac arrived at the London screening of *High School Musical 3: Senior Year* in a fitted black suit and tie.

Zac's Star Style

Zac has a look that is all his own. His signature layered hairstyle adds to his heartthrob appeal. He prefers jeans and a T-shirt. But on the red carpet, Zac wears classic suits in colors like black, gray, or silver. At the 2007 MTV Movie Awards, he wore a metallic gray suit with a skinny tie. The 2007 Teen Choice Awards found Zac in black pants and vest over a short-sleeved white T-shirt. Formal or casual, Zac always gets it right.

Growing up Zac

Zachary David Alexander Efron was born October 18, 1987, in San Luis Obispo, California. Zac's parents, David and Starla, met at a power plant where they both worked. They welcomed a second son, Dylan, four years after Zac was born. The Efrons raised their sons in the nearby town of Arroyo Grande. The close-knit family also includes two Australian shepherds, Dreamer and Puppy, and a Siamese cat named Simon.

Head of the Class

Education was important in the Efron household. Zac had to finish his homework before he could relax. But he didn't mind his parents' strict policy on getting good grades. Zac considered himself a bookworm. He studied hard and earned straight As on his report cards. Zac's favorite class was English.

Once he finished his schoolwork, Zac got to have fun. He liked playing video games and skateboarding with his friends. Zac, Dylan, and their dad often went to see the San Francisco Giants play baseball. They showed up for games early to watch practice and catch foul balls. Zac's autographed baseball collection is his prized possession.

Zac, shown here at age 13, attended Arroyo Grande High School in Arroyo Grande, California.

Zac also loved playing sports. He joined Little League baseball and his school's basketball team. But to his disappointment, he was not a star athlete.

Star Talents

Zac would never be a professional athlete, but he had other talents. Zac could listen to a song on the radio and memorize the words. He could then sing it back in perfect pitch. Zac made up silly songs before he went to bed. He watched musicals like *Grease* and *Singin' in the Rain*. Then he acted out his favorite parts. Zac's parents took note of his talent. They signed him up for singing and piano lessons. Next, they guided him toward the stage.

At age 11, Zac auditioned for the role of a newsboy in the play *Gypsy*. Zac won the part. *Gypsy* ran for 90 performances at the Pacific Conservatory of Performing Arts in Santa Maria, California. Zac soon became hooked on acting. He enjoyed making people laugh and hearing the applause. He acted in other plays, such as *Peter Pan* and *Little Shop of Horrors*. Zac impressed his middle school acting teacher, and she referred him to an agent.

"My dad convinced me to go out and audition for my first play. I went kicking and screaming, but little did I know my dad had just showed me the coolest thing on earth."

— Zac, from an interview with *Scholastic News Online*.

Zac, shown here at age 16, was a natural at stage acting.

Zac lived at home with his parents in Arroyo Grande, California, until he turned 19.

Growing Pains

After Zac signed with his agent, his mom drove him to Los Angeles for TV and movie auditions. They spent six hours in the car, round trip, for each audition. Because of his stage experience, Zac often **projected** his voice. At his first big audition, he shouted during a tender moment in the script. Zac blew the audition. Because of his inexperience, Zac was rejected from many other auditions.

Zac began to wonder if the auditions were worth his time. His mother was tired of the long drives. It was hard for Zac to miss school. To keep up his good grades, Zac studied overtime. He even mailed homework to his teachers. Finally Zac's parents told him he had to get some roles or give up acting. But Zac enjoyed acting too much to quit. In 2002 he made a small guest appearance on the TV show *Firefly*. Appearances on *ER* and *The Guardian* soon followed.

project — to make your voice carry very far

A Breakout Star

Zac's acting career heated up in 2004. He landed a role on the TV drama *Summerland*. Zac played Cameron Bale, the physically abused son of an alcoholic. At first, Zac made small guest appearances. The show's writers liked his work. They developed the part, and Zac became a regular cast member.

While working on *Summerland*, Zac took on another tough role. He played a boy with **autism** in the TV movie *Miracle Run*. The Lifetime original movie starred Mary-Louise Parker as a single mother raising autistic twins. Zac played Steven, the twin who wants to be a runner. Critics said his performance had depth and heart. Zac was nominated for Best Supporting Young Actor by the Young Artist Foundation.

autism — a condition that causes people to have trouble communicating and forming relationships with others

Zac played an autistic runner in the TV movie *Miracle Run*.

Zac (back row, second from left) joined the cast of *Summerland* in 2004.

Summerland was cancelled in 2005. But Zac's disappointment didn't last long. That year he played a Derby Cup rider in the film *The Derby Stallion*. Zac had to learn how to ride a horse for the role. After three lessons, Zac got his horse to do jumps and sprints. Zac did his own riding in most of the horseback scenes. *The Derby Stallion* did not show in theaters. Still, Zac's experience and hard work were about to pay off.

High School Musical

Soon after filming *The Derby Stallion*, Zac learned he would play Troy Bolton in *High School Musical*. Zac flew straight to Salt Lake City, Utah, where the movie would be filmed. For six hot summer weeks, Zac and the cast lived at the Little America Hotel in Salt Lake City.

Zac and the cast rehearsed for weeks to perform numbers such as "Get'cha Head in the Game."

Director Kenny Ortega (far left) gave direction to Zac and Vanessa during filming.

Practice Makes Perfect

The *HSM* cast rehearsed for two weeks before filming began. They practiced for up to eight hours each day. In a mirror-lined dance studio, Zac learned complex dance routines. He sang and danced while dribbling a basketball for numbers like "Get'cha Head in the Game." Even without formal dance training, Zac kept up with the professionals. He even skipped breaks to cram in as much practice as possible.

Zac's dedication impressed his director, Kenny Ortega. Anyone caught yawning had to pay Ortega a dollar. Zac worked long hours but didn't tire easily. Ortega didn't earn big bucks from Zac.

"The only thing that separates me from 200 brown-haired, blue-eyed guys in L.A. is one single audition. I'll never forget that."

— Zac from an interview with *Time* magazine.

On the Set

Once rehearsals were over, filming began. Filmmakers shot the movie in 28 days at a real high school in Salt Lake City. Hundreds of movie extras filled the set. Filming lasted 14 to 16 hours each day.

After long hours on set, Zac and the cast kicked back. They swam in the pool, ate in restaurants, and toured Salt Lake City. When the movie wrapped, everyone was sad to go home. Filming had been as fun as summer camp. Zac had no idea that his little made-for-TV movie was about to become a huge hit.

A Big Debut

HSM **premiered** on the Disney Channel in January 2006. With 7.7 million viewers, it was the most-watched Disney Channel movie ever. Zac's fame shot into orbit. Google hits for Zac Efron numbered in the millions. Soon Zac appeared on the covers of teen magazines. At first Zac didn't think fame would change his life. Then he tried to go see a movie and got mobbed by fans. He had to get used to his new superstar status.

Back to School

HSM led to a best-selling album, a concert tour, an ice show, a book series, a TV reality show, and two sequels. In *High School Musical 2*, the friends worked at a resort during summer vacation. Zac learned how to golf for the film. When *HSM2* debuted in August 2007, 17.2 million people tuned in. Fans made *HSM2* the most-watched cable show ever. *High School Musical 3: Senior Year* featured prom and graduation. *HSM3* became the first of the hit series to open in theaters in October 2008. The film earned $42 million its opening weekend.

With all his acting success, Zac never forgot his studies. He graduated from Arroyo Grande High School in June 2006.

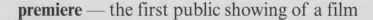

premiere — the first public showing of a film

Zac attended the *HSM* DVD premiere with (left to right) Kaycee Stroh, Lucas Grabeel, Ashley Tisdale, Chris Warren, Bob Chapek, Vanessa Hudgens, and Monique Coleman.

The Red Carpet

The *High School Musical* DVD release was so huge that it got a Hollywood premiere. On May 13, 2006, Zac walked the red carpet looking cool in an aqua T-shirt and jeans. He wore a star necklace given to him by Paula Abdul. He smiled and waved at screaming fans. The El Capitan Theatre showed the sing-along version of the movie. The after party had karaoke and a station to make your own video. Tables were decorated with pom-poms and basketballs in red and white, the East High Wildcat colors.

Hollywood Calls

Starring in *High School Musical* led to other Hollywood roles for Zac. He put his singing and dancing skills back to use in the 2007 musical *Hairspray*. Celebs Michelle Pfeiffer, Queen Latifah, and John Travolta also starred in the film. Zac played Link Larkin, the ultra-cool teen star of a hit dance show. To become Link, Zac cut and darkened his hair. He even gained 15 pounds. *Hairspray* rehearsals lasted two and a half months. The cast and crew filmed for another six months.

Hairspray premiered in Los Angeles, Baltimore, New York City, London, and Sydney. Zac hit the red carpets in classic suits and metallic ties. *Hairspray* was later nominated for Best Motion Picture – Musical or Comedy at the 2008 Golden Globe Awards.

Excited fans greeted Zac at the Los Angeles premiere of *Hairspray*.

"In the 1960s, the clothes were very tight. I didn't want chicken legs."
— Zac on why he gained weight for *Hairspray*, from an interview with *Moviefone*.

New Challenges

Zac enjoyed making musicals. But he wanted to challenge himself by acting in different types of movies. In April 2009, Zac appeared in the film *17 Again*. He played Mike, an unhappy man in his 30s who gets to relive high school. To play an older man trapped in a younger body, Zac acted like his dad. Matthew Perry from *Friends* costarred as the adult Mike.

Also out in 2009 was *Me and Orson Welles*. Zac played Richard, a new actor who works with famed director Orson Welles. The film is set in New York City in 1937. It was a perfect role for Zac who loves old Hollywood movies.

Zac and *Hairspray* costar Nikki Blonsky became good friends on set.

Strong Work Ethic

Zac's strong work ethic sets him apart from many other young Hollywood actors. He takes time to learn more about the characters he plays. Zac respects his directors and listens to their advice. He asks for extra takes to make sure his performances are perfect. Zac arrives early to interviews, where he is polite and well-spoken.

Life in Hollywood

Zac loves his fans. When he is out in public, he signs autographs and poses for snapshots. But he also tries to keep his private life private. Zac avoids celeb hangouts that attract crowds of **paparazzi**. He disguises his good looks with sunglasses and a hat. Zac has admitted to dating his *HSM* costar Vanessa Hudgens. But he tries not to comment about his personal relationships.

Stardom does have its perks. Zac got a surprise when he appeared on *The Tonight Show* in August 2007. Jay Leno gave him a baseball signed by his hero, Giants star Barry Bonds. A few weeks later, Zac got to meet Bonds before a game. And don't forget the cash. According to *Forbes* magazine, Zac earned $5.8 million from June 2007 to June 2008.

Hair Care

In the film *Hairspray*, Zac and the gang showered each other with hairspray during many musical numbers. Zac revealed that those spray cans were actually full of deodorant! The deodorant was more visible on camera than actual hairspray. The cast had to wash off the deodorant spray after each take. Talk about a hair-tastrophe!

paparazzi — aggressive photographers who take pictures of celebrities for sale to magazines or newspapers

CHAPTER 5

A Regular Guy

With all of his success, Zac insists he's just a regular guy. He still hangs out in Arroyo Grande and stays in touch with hometown friends. For his 21st birthday, Zac enjoyed a quiet dinner out with family and close friends. When Zac first moved to Los Angeles, he rented a small apartment. He recently purchased his first home. Zac likes living on his own but misses his mom's cooking.

Zac's schedule is packed with auditions, movies, interviews, and red-carpet events. When he's not at work, Zac likes to stay active. He eats healthful foods and exercises regularly. He surfs, skis, snowboards, and skateboards. He also goes golfing and rock climbing.

Zac spends his free time exercising, playing sports, and hanging out with family and friends.

In December 2008, Zac delivered gifts to patients at the Mattel Children's Hospital in Los Angeles, California.

Giving Back

As soon as Zac gained fame, he started donating time and money to charities. He visited children's hospitals with his *High School Musical* costars. In 2007, he delivered donated school supplies to John Adams Middle School in Los Angeles. Students got a real treat when Zac stuck around to talk to them about DonorsChoose.org. This agency helps provide public schools with much-needed supplies. He also golfed at the 2007 Dennis Quaid Charity Weekend to raise money for children's health care.

Future Plans

Zac's future plans include acting and college. In the works for Zac is a film version of the book *The Death and Life of Charlie St. Cloud*. The story is about a cemetery caretaker who feels responsible for his younger brother's death. *17 Again* director Burr Steers is set to direct the flick.

Zac has also been accepted into the University of Southern California. He plans to study film. But Zac has put off college for now. Too many good film roles are coming his way. Zac hopes to star in an action film and would like to go behind the camera to direct.

Zac Efron made his transition from teen star to mature actor look easy. What's next for this rising star? Movie critics and fans try to predict his next career move, but only Zac can decide. One thing is clear – whatever this superstar chooses will take him straight to the top.

Zac's Awards

- **"Best Breakout Star"** at the 2006 Teen Choice Awards. Zac and *High School Musical* costar Vanessa Hudgens also won an award for "Best Chemistry."
- **"The One to Watch"** at the 2007 Young Hollywood Awards for his performance in *Hairspray*.
- **"Breakthrough Performance"** at the 2008 MTV Movie Awards for his role as Link Larkin in *Hairspray*.

Glossary

agent (AY-juhnt) — someone who helps actors find work

alcoholic (al-kuh-HOL-ik) — a person who has a disease that makes it difficult not to drink alcohol even when drinking hurts his or her body, mind, or ability to function

audition (aw-DISH-uhn) — a tryout performance for an actor

autism (AW-tiss-uhm) — a condition that causes people to have trouble communicating and forming relationships with others; they may have difficulty with language.

ethic (ETH-ik) — a belief in doing what is right

paparazzi (pah-puh-RAHT-see) — aggressive photographers who take pictures of celebrities for sale to magazines or newspapers

policy (POL-uh-see) — a general plan or principle that people use to help them make decisions or take action

premiere (pri-MIHR) — the first public performance of a film, play, or work of music or dance

project (pruh-JEKT) — to make your voice carry very far

take (TAYK) — the filming of a TV or movie scene

Read More

Jones, Jen. *Being Famous.* 10 Things You Need to Know About. Mankato, Minn.: Capstone Press, 2008.

Keedle, Jayne. *Zac Efron.* Today's Superstars: Entertainment. Pleasantville, N.Y.: Gareth Stevens, 2009.

Riddolls, Tom, and Judy Wearing. *Zac Efron.* Remarkable People. New York: Weigl Publishers, 2010.

Saunders, Catherine. *High School Musical: The Essential Guide.* New York: DK, 2008.

Internet Sites

FactHound offers a safe, fun way to find Internet sites related to this book. All of the sites on FactHound have been researched by our staff.

Here's all you do:

Visit *www.facthound.com*

FactHound will fetch the best sites for you!

Index